Dave Lambert

Make a difference

An Action UK! film script

Ernst Klett Verlag
Stuttgart · Leipzig

Acknowledgement:
The Oxfam logo and the Oxfam copyright name are used with the permission of Oxfam GB, Oxfam House, John Smith Drive, Cowley, Oxford OX4 2JY, UK www.oxfam.org.uk . Oxfam GB does not necessarily endorse any text or activities that accompany the materials.

1. Auflage 1 7 6 5 4 3 | 2017 16 15 14 13

Illustrationen: Steffen Wolff, Düsseldorf sowie Christian Dekelver, Weinstadt
Druck: AZ Druck und Datentechnik GmbH, Kempten/Allgäu

Printed in Germany.
ISBN 978-3-12-547090-3

9 783125 470903

Contents

Make a difference – An Action UK! film script

Main characters

Josh [dʒɒʃ]
wants to lead, serious but still has a sense of humour, can be arrogant, loves to make films

Maya ['maɪə]
organizes the group, sometimes emotional, talks to people well, has a sense of humour, thinks of good ideas

Greg [greg]
likes sport, loves to eat, sometimes easily influenced, friendly, gets scared easily

Havana [hə'vænə] *(a new friend)*
creative, enthusiastic, likes to explain things, liked by everyone

Other characters

Maya's gran	Old woman
Maya's mum	Old man
Maya's dad	Housewife
Stacey ['steɪsi]	Young mother
Mrs Burns	Blind girl
Greg's mum	Young man
Greg's dad	First buyer
Young boy	Second buyer
Angry woman	Coach

to make a difference [meɪk ə 'dɪfrns] etw. verändern, etw. bewegen • **film script** [fɪlm skrɪpt] Drehbuch • **main character** [meɪn 'kærəktə] Hauptdarsteller • **sense of humour** [ˌsens əv 'hju:mə] Sinn für Humor • **arrogant** ['ærəgənt] arrogant • **emotional** [ɪ'məʊʃnl] emotional • **easily influenced** [ˌi:zɪli 'ɪnfluənst] leicht beeinflussbar • **creative** [kri'eɪtɪv] kreativ • **enthusiastic** [ɪnˌθju:zi'æstɪk] begeistert • **gran** [græn] Oma • **Coach** [kəʊtʃ] Trainer

Before you read the script

1 The title

Part of the title of this film script is 'Make a Difference'.

a) *Explain what you think this part means.*

b) *How do you think you can 'make a difference' (in your school, your town, etc.)?*

2 Cover picture

In groups of 3, look at the cover picture.

a) *Talk about what you think has happened.*

b) *Compare your ideas with another group.*

3 The characters

Read about the main characters Josh, Maya, Greg and Havana on p 4. Which character do you think …

a) … is probably the most organized person?
b) … prefers to watch a film than play football?
c) … prefers to play football than watch a film?
d) … probably likes to interview people?
e) … would probably be a good teacher?
f) … is hungry most often?
g) … is sometimes too proud?
h) … usually wants to follow other people's ideas?
i) … doesn't usually want to follow other people's ideas?
j) … probably likes to draw and to dance?

probably ['prɒbəbli] vermutlich • **to prefer** [prɪ'fɜː] vorziehen • **would** [wʊd] würde • **proud** [praʊd] stolz

4 What is Oxfam?

Work with a partner. Go to www.oxfam.org.uk. Look at 'Oxfam in action' and fill in the information.

This website is from a ____________ called Oxfam. It helps ________ people all over the world in countries like _________ and _________. Oxfam sells things like _________ in its second-hand shop and collects _________ to pay for projects to help these people. But these are just two examples of Oxfam's fundraising ideas. Oxfam's projects help people in many ways. For example, some projects help people who are hungry to get ____________ and people who are ill to get _____________.

5 Sounds and dialogues

People use sounds to show what they think or feel. Work with a partner. Make these sounds to show these meanings.

Sounds	**Meaning**
Hmmm.	You're thinking.
Huh?	You're surprised or you don't understand.
Oh?/Oh!	You're surprised./You're unhappy.
Er .../Um ...	You're thinking before speaking.
Oops!/Uh-oh!	Something went wrong.
Ugh!	Something is terrible.
Mmmm!	You like something (often food); you agree with someone.
Wow!	You're surprised, excited.
Ha (ha)!	You find something funny./You're being sarcastic.

Oxfam ['ɒksfæm] *Hilfsorganisation* • **fundraising** ['fʌndˌreɪzɪŋ] Wohltätigkeits-, Benefiz- • **way** [weɪ] Weise • **Huh?** [hʌ] • **Oh? Oh!** [əʊ] • **Er ...** [ɜː] • **Um ...** [əm] • **Oops!** [uːps] • **Uh-oh!** [ʌəʊ] • **Ugh!** [ʌg] • **Wow!** [waʊ]

SCENE 1. INTERIOR. SCHOOL. DAY.

Year 11B are coming out of the school hall. Mrs Burns has shown them a film about Africa. Outside the hall there is a poster for the film. Some pupils are putting money in the donation box. Maya, Josh, Greg and Havana are standing by the poster.

MAYA: That was an interesting film. *(looks at poster)* 'SOS Africa'. It really makes you think!

HAVANA: Yeah. Some people in Africa are so poor and hungry!

GREG: Yeah, they're starving.

MAYA: Last night I had too many chips … I couldn't eat them all. So I threw them away. Now I feel bad … .

---

interior [ɪnˈtɪəriə] innen • 1 **to come out** [kʌm ˈaʊt] herauskommen • 4 **donation box** [dəˈneɪʃn bɒks] Spendenbox • **Picture annotations: famine** [ˈfæmɪn] Hungersnot • **poverty** [ˈpɒvəti] Armut • 10 **to starve** [stɑːv] verhungern • 12 **to feel bad** [fiːl ˈbæd] ein schlechtes Gewissen haben

Havana: I know what you mean, Maya. It really isn't fair. We have too much food … .

Maya: And they don't have enough.

Greg: Hmmm. I'll never say 'I'm starving' again!

Josh: I don't understand why Mrs Burns showed us a film like that. Africa's so far away. The problems are so big. We can't really do anything to help … .

Maya: We can do something, Josh. We can give money.

Havana: The film said some Africans have less than 50p a day! Imagine!

Greg: But that's not possible, Havana! You can't even buy a sandwich in the school cafeteria for 50p!

Josh: I still don't see how we can 'save' Africa.

Maya: Well, I'm donating my pocket money to this charity.

Havana: Me, too. *(Maya and Havana put some coins in the donation box. They look at Greg and wait for him to do the same.)*

Greg: Huh? OK. Here, I'll give something, too. *(Greg puts some coins in the donation box.)*

Josh: Now I feel bad … .

Havana/Maya: Why Josh?

Josh: Well, my pocket money is £4 a week. Last night I complained to my mum that it wasn't enough … .

Josh puts some money in the box. Sound of the school bell.

Greg: *(suddenly happy)* Come on guys, that's the bell for lunch! I'm starving!

Greg runs off. The others look surprised and shake their heads.

---

9 **the film said** [ðə fɪlm 'sed] im Film wird behauptet, dass • 14 **to donate** [də'neɪt] spenden • 15 **coin** [kɔɪn] Münze • 25 **Come on** [kʌm‿'ɒn] Kommt! • 27 **to run off** [rʌn‿'ɒf] weglaufen, wegrennen

SCENE 2. INTERIOR. JOSH'S HOUSE. EVENING.

Josh is having supper with his mother in the dining room.

JOSH: We watched a film in school today, Mum.

JOSH'S MUM: *(serving dinner)* Oh? Here you are, Josh.

JOSH: Sausages, great! Thanks, Mum. The film was about Africa.

MUM: Oh, that's nice … .

JOSH: It wasn't nice at all, Mum! Some Africans kids are so poor, they don't have enough clothes to wear. They don't even have books for school.

MUM: *(looks sad)* Yes, there is a lot of poverty there.

JOSH: I don't understand why they show us films like that. What can I do? It only makes you depressed. We all donated some money, but how much can that help?

MUM: Your grandfather came from Africa, you know?

JOSH: Where exactly in Africa did he come from, Mum?

MUM: From a country called Sudan.

JOSH: Oh! The film was all about Sudan. It looks like a beautiful country, but the people are so poor!

MUM: I know, dear. It's so unfair. It really makes you want to do something, doesn't it?

JOSH: Yeah, but what?

MUM: *(thinking)* Well, you found out about the problem in Africa because you watched a film –

JOSH: And?

MUM: Well, Josh, I thought you wanted to be a famous film director … .

JOSH: I do! But I can't go to Africa and direct a film, can I Mum?

MUM: No, but you could make a film here and make a difference.

JOSH: *(thinking)* Hmmm … make a film and make a difference. But how?

---

3 **to serve** [sɜːv] servieren • 7 **kid** [kɪd] Jugendliche/-r • 12 **depressed** [dɪ'prest] depremiert • 19 **dear** [dɪə] Schatz • 25 **film director** [fɪlm dɪ'rektə] Regisseur

SCENE 3. INTERIOR. MAYA'S HOUSE. EVENING.

Maya is having supper with her parents and younger sister.

MAYA'S MUM: I took Pushkin to the vet's today. *(speaks to the cat under the table in a funny voice)* Yes, did you like the vet's, Pushkin?

STACEY: *(laughing)* Mum! Hello! Er … you're talking to the cat again!

MUM: He understands me, Stacey. *(to the cat)* Don't you, Pushkin? Yes, that's right, you do!

DAD: The vet's? What's wrong with Pushkin?

MUM: The poor thing's too fat. He eats too much. Soon he won't be able to get through his cat flap! *(They all laugh, but Maya is serious.)*

MAYA: Mum? You took Pushkin to the vet's because he's too fat?

MUM: He's already on a diet, but you know Pushkin, he always wants more. You'd think he was starving! I had to buy some medicine to stop his appetite. The visit to the vet's cost £55.

MAYA: *(talking to herself)* Children in Africa are starving because they don't have enough food … and they're sick because there isn't enough medicine. And we buy expensive medicine for our cat because he eats too much?

The doorbell rings.

MAYA: That's Havana. Bye everyone!

Maya gets up from the table and runs out of the room.

MUM: Maya! Oh, she hasn't eaten her potatoes again!

---

3 **the vet's** [ðə 'vetz] Tierarztpraxis • 10 **What's wrong** [wʌtz 'rɒŋ] Was ist los? • 11 **soon** [suːn] bald • 12 **cat flap** ['kæt flæp] Katzentür • 17 **you'd think …** [jud 'θɪŋk] man könnte meinen, dass … • 22 **sick** [sɪk] krank

SCENE 4. INTERIOR. SCHOOL. NIGHT.

Havana is waiting across the hall from the locker room to walk home with Greg.

GREG: *(coming out of the locker room)* Oh, hi Havana. How was music club?

HAVANA: Cool! We're learning to play the drums. Listen!

She drums on the wall with her hands. While she's doing this, the coach goes into the locker room behind them, but they don't see or hear him.

GREG: Wow! That's great!

HAVANA: Thanks! How was football practice?

GREG: Great. Come on, let's go. I'm the last one to leave the locker room.

HAVANA: Wait, Greg. If there's no one else in there … why are all the lights still on?

GREG: Huh? I don't know … come on, Havana.

HAVANA: Turn the lights off, Greg.

GREG: Why?

HAVANA: Don't you remember what the film said?

GREG: Er … no?

HAVANA: "When the earth gets hotter, Africa really feels it."

GREG: Huh? If we leave the lights on in the locker room, how can it be bad for Africa?

HAVANA: A lot of the energy we use puts more CO_2 into the air, and more CO_2 leads to global warming, right?

GREG: Right … .

HAVANA: For example there's less rain in many areas of Africa, and global warming is making this worse. Without rain, all the plant life dies … .

---

1 **locker room** ['lɒkə ru:m] Umkleideraum • 6 **to drum on** ['drʌm ɒn] trommeln an • 20 **earth** [ɜ:θ] Erde • 20 **really feels it** [rɪəli 'fi:lz‿ɪt] ist stark davon betroffen • 23 **energy** ['enədʒi] Energie • 24 **global warming** [ˌgləʊbl 'wɔ:mɪŋ] globale Erwärmung • 28 **plant life** ['plɑ:nt laɪf] Pflanzenwelt

Greg: *(remembering the film)* So there isn't any food for the animals or the people. You're right!

Greg opens the door to the locker room and turns the lights off.

Havana: That's better!

Coach: (*from inside the locker room)* Hey! Who turned the lights off?

Greg: The Coach is in there!

Havana: Uh-oh!

Greg and Havana run away.

SCENE 5. INTERIOR. SCHOOL. DAY.

The four friends are standing outside the school hall. Maya, Havana are looking at the SOS Africa poster. Greg is holding a football and Josh is looking at photos on his camera.

Maya: You know, guys, that film Mrs Burns showed us yesterday about Africa has really made me think.

Havana: Me too, Maya!

Maya: For example, my mum took our cat to the vet's –

Havana: Is Pushkin sick?

Maya: No, he's just too fat. He eats too much.

Greg: That's crazy! Africans are starving and English cats have too much to eat?

Maya: I know. And it cost £55! Think how much medicine that money could buy for poor African kids!

Josh: Yeah, and I could be one of them … .

Greg, Maya, Havana: What? Huh? What do you mean, Josh?

Josh: *(puts his camera away.)* Well, I knew my mum's father was African … but last night she told me he came from Sudan.

Greg: That's the country in the film, isn't it?

6 **Hey!** [heɪ] He! • 24 **could be** [ˈkʊd bi] könnte sein

HAVANA: The place where some parents can't buy books for their kids to go to school …

MAYA: … or food to eat, or medicines to take when they're sick.

JOSH: Yeah, that's the place my grandfather came from. Imagine, if he had stayed there, I could be one of those kids! That could be me, guys!

MAYA: God! It makes you understand how lucky we are.

HAVANA: And how unlucky the poor people in Sudan are. Come on, we'll be late for French.

While they walk along the hall, Greg turns off the lights.

JOSH: Er … Greg, what are you doing?

GREG: I'm turning off the lights, Josh. Don't you remember what the film said? "When the earth gets hotter –

HAVANA and MAYA: Africa really feels it!"

JOSH: *(thinking)* You mean my relatives in Africa really feel it!

SCENE 6. EXTERIOR. SCHOOL. PLAYGROUND.

Greg, Maya and Josh are sitting on a bench in the lunch break. Havana runs towards them and sits down.

HAVANA: *(excited)* Guys, listen! You know we were all talking about making a difference in Africa?

MAYA: Yeah!

JOSH and GREG: *(unsure of what Havana is going say)* Hmmm … er … yeah?

HAVANA: Well, if we really want to make a difference … we should start our own charity!

JOSH: Start our own charity? Get real, Havana. We can't start our own charity!

---

3 **to take medicine** [teɪk ˈmedsn] Medikament einnehmen • 6 **if he had stayed there** [ˌɪfˈhi həd ˈsteɪd ðeə] wenn er dort geblieben wäre • 11 **along** [əˈlɒŋ] entlang • **exterior** [ɪkˈstɪəriə] außen • 27 **Get real!** [ɡet ˈrɪəl] Bleib auf dem Teppich!

Havana: The people who started Oxfam did. They lived in Oxford and they wanted to make a difference.

Maya: Just like us!

Havana: Right, Maya. They wanted to stop famine.

Greg: *(thinking)* The word Oxford … plus famine … equals Oxfam! So that's where they got the cool name.

Havana: The original name was "Oxford Committee for Famine Relief". Oxfam have a shop near Greenwich. It sells cool second-hand clothes and stuff. The money goes to help the poor.

Maya: Guys, if we start our own charity too, we'll really change things!

Havana: *(marching left and right)* Stop famine now!

Maya: *(marching with Havana)* Yeah, stop world poverty!

Havana: Stop global warming!

Maya: SOS Africa!

Havana: Feed the world!

Greg: *(jumps up and marches with the girls)* Yeah! Feed the world, but with no packaging!

The girls stop marching and look at Greg, surprised.

Greg: What's wrong? *(stops marching)* Our food comes in too much packaging! It's bad for the environment. So, no more packaging!

Maya: *(smiling)* What, Greg, no packaging at all?

Greg: No!

Maya: Hmmm. But what about eggs, Greg?

Greg: Huh?

Maya: Eggs, Greg. Well, they'd break if there was no packaging at all.

Greg: Well … *(starts marching again)* No more packaging except for eggs!

They all laugh at Greg.

---

7 **original** [əˈrɪdʒnl] ursprünglich • 7 **committee** [kəˈmɪti] Ausschuss, Komitee • 8 **relief** [rɪˈliːf] Hilfe • 10 **goes to help the poor** [gəʊz tə ˌhelp ðə ˈpɔː] kommt den Armen zugute • 19 **packaging** [ˈpækɪdʒɪŋ] Verpackung • 22 **environment** [ɪnˈvaɪrnmənt] Umwelt • 28 **they'd (= they would)** [ðeɪd] sie würden

JOSH: *(dreaming)* Hmmm. Our own charity! Maybe it's not a bad idea . . . . We could become famous like those Oxfam people. We must have a meeting to talk about this.

MAYA: Hey Josh, this isn't about becoming famous … it's about helping Africa, OK?

JOSH: I know that, Maya. *(to Greg and Havana)* Let's have a meeting today after school.

GREG: OK. Where? A charity needs headquarters.

JOSH: Hmmm … I know! The headquarters can be my bedroom!

SCENE 7. INTERIOR. JOSH'S BEDROOM. DAY.

Havana and Maya are on Josh's bed. Greg is sitting on the floor. Josh is standing in front of them. On the wall behind him is a small whiteboard.

9 **headquarters** [ˌhedˈkwɔːtəz] Hauptsitz • 13 **whiteboard** [ˈwaɪtbɔːd] Tafel, auf die man mit abwischbarem Stift schreibt

JOSH: Good afternoon ladies and gentlemen and welcome to our first meeting. For a start, our charity needs a good name. Any ideas from the committee?

MAYA: *(laughs)* How about Josh's Brilliant Charity? Ha!

JOSH: Very funny, Maya! Hmmm. Our name must be something people can remember. The Committee for … *(He writes on the whiteboard.)*

MAYA: The Committee for…. African … er …

GREG: The Committee for African Support …

HAVANA: … and Help! The Committee for African Support and Help!

MAYA: It's a great name, but no one will be able to remember it. It's too long.

HAVANA: *(jumps up and cleans the whiteboard, but leaves only the first letter of each word)* But they'll remember this! C-A-S-H. Cash!

MAYA: Brilliant, Havana! There's just one more thing missing … . *(She goes to the whiteboard and makes the S into a $.)*

JOSH: Great ideas, everyone!

They all clap.

MAYA: Now we need to decide on our roles on the committee.

GREG: I think Havana should make a poster. She's a brilliant designer.

JOSH: Does the committee agree?

They all raise their hands.

JOSH: OK. The CA$H poster designer is Havana.

HAVANA: I think Maya should be our secretary.

MAYA: Secretary? Why me?

HAVANA: Because you're such a fast writer, Maya. Who votes for Maya as secretary?

---

1 **ladies and gentlemen** ['leɪdiz‿ən‿dʒentlmən] meine Damen und Herren • 2 **for a start** [fər‿ə 'stɑ:t] erst einmal, für den Anfang • 9 **support** [sə'pɔ:t] Unterstützung • 16 **cash** [kæʃ] Bargeld • 27 **to raise** [reɪz] heben • 32 **as** [əz] als

They raise their hands.

Josh: OK. The secretary is Maya.

Maya: Who is going to be our chairperson?

They all look at each other.

Greg: Well, Havana is our poster designer, and Maya is our secretary. I don't want to be the chairperson … so that only leaves you, Josh.

Josh: *(very happy)* Thank you, Greg. Does everyone agree?

They raise their hands.

Josh: So I am chairperson. Now –

Greg: Hey, what about me? What's my role?

They try to think of a role for Greg, but no one can.

Greg: *(happy)* Hey, I can serve the food!

Maya: What food? The committee doesn't serve food! That's all you think about, Greg!

Josh: Don't worry, Greg, I'll need you as my PA.

Greg: Huh? PA?

Josh: My personal assistant. Does everyone agree?

They raise their hands.

Josh: Greg is the Chairperson's PA! Now, please remember that CA$H is top secret! No one outside this committee must know our plans.

Havana: Er … Josh? How can we help and support Africa if no one knows about us?

Josh: We don't want other charities to steal our plans, Havana!

Havana: Oh, of course not!

Greg: Er … guys? What are our plans?

They look at each other, but no one has a plan.

---

3 **chairperson** [ˈtʃeəˌpɜːsn] Vorsitzende/-r • 7 **to leave** [liːv] *(hier)* übrig bleiben • 18 **personal assistant** [ˌpɜːsnl əˈsɪstnt] persönliche/-r Assistent/-in • 21 **top secret** [tɒp ˈsiːkrət] streng geheim • 27 **of course not** [əv ˈkɔːs nɒt] natürlich nicht

Maya: Um … let's all go home and do some serious thinking!

SCENE 8. INTERIOR. GREG'S HOUSE. EVENING.

Greg and Havana are sitting on the sofa in Greg's living room and are watching TV.

Greg: My favourite programme!

Havana: Oh, let's not watch TV, Greg, let's think about our charity. *(She makes notes in an exercise book.)*

Greg: Relax. *(looks at the TV)* Ugh! Sebastiano! I hate him! He gets so much money … .

Havana: That's what we need to do: raise money!

Greg: *(He hasn't heard Havana.)* He can't act, he can't sing. Why is he always on TV and in magazines? Why is *Sebastiano* famous and *I'm* not?

Havana: *(laughs)* Because he's sooo cute! Hey! That's what we need!

Greg: Huh? What?

Havana: A celebrity! We need someone cute and famous to help our charity. Like Sebastiano! Thanks Greg, you have brilliant ideas!

Greg: I do?

A split scene: on the left, Havana opens her mobile and calls Maya. Greg is sitting beside her and is listening. On the right is Maya (also sitting on a sofa, reading a magazine). Her mobile rings and she answers.

Maya: Hi Havana, what's up?

Havana: Maya! Greg and I have just had a brainwave for our charity!

---

1 **to do some serious thinking** [də sʌm ˌsɪəriəs ˈθɪŋkɪŋ] ernsthaft über etw. nachdenken • 8 **Sebastiano** [seˈbæstiænə] • 10 **to raise money** [reɪz ˈmʌni] Geld sammeln • 21 **split scene** [splɪt ˈsiːn] geteilte Bühne • 24 **to answer (the telephone)** [ˈɑːnsə] ans Telefon gehen • 25 **What's up?** [wɒts‿ˈʌp] Was gibt's Neues? • 26 **brainwave** [ˈbreɪnweɪv] Geistesblitz

Maya: Yeah, what is it?
Havana: We need a celebrity!
Maya: A celebrity? Wow! You mean someone famous and talented and cute like … like … Sebastiano?
Havana: Mmmm! Yes! I'm going to contact celebrities on their websites now!
Greg: *(to himself)* Oh nooo. Now what have I started … ?

SCENE 9. INTERIOR. JOSH'S BEDROOM. DAY.

The committee is sitting on Josh's bedroom floor.

Josh: So, thanks for coming to the committee's second meeting, everyone. Did you contact any celebrities on the Internet, Havana?
Greg: Yeah, but no one answered, not even the lovely Sebastiano, ha ha!
Maya: *(angry)* Be quiet, Greg. *(to Havana)* Never mind, Havana, you tried.
Josh: Has anybody got any other brainwaves for how we can raise money?
Maya: Well, most charities like Oxfam raise money by selling second-hand things.
Greg: Yeah, what can we sell?
Maya: Why don't we do like Oxfam and sell unwanted clothes too?
Greg: Cool!
Havana: I think we should e-mail everyone we know, all our friends, all the school!
Josh: Secretary Maya, please write this e-mail. Let me see: "Dear friends! …"
Maya: *(laughs)* Just a minute, please! Let me get to your laptop! *(moves to the desk)* OK, ready!

14 **Never mind!** [ˌnevə ˈmaɪnd] Mach dir nichts draus! • 21 **unwanted** [ʌnˈwɒntɪd] *(hier)* abgelegt

Josh: *(thinking as he talks)* "Dear Friends! Dear School! We are a new charity called CA$H. If you want to make a difference in Africa, open your wardrobes, take out the clothes you don't want and bring them to … ." *(pauses)* to where?

Maya: Hmmm. We don't have a shop. Where can people bring their unwanted clothes?

Havana: Why not here, to our headquarters?

Josh: What! This is my bedroom! Where will I sleep? Why don't we collect the clothes in your garage, Greg?

Greg: What? My mum and dad will go mental!

Havana: But we'll need a collection point, Greg. Your place is perfect for it, it's so central … .

Greg looks very worried.

Josh: Oh please, Greggy, it'll only be for a few days. I thought you wanted to make a difference … .

Greg: I do but –

All: Thanks, Greg!

Maya: I'll send an e-mail to everyone and tell them to bring their unwanted clothes to Greg's address. Just for a short time. How about from Sunday night to Wednesday night?

Josh: OK, Maya, but wait for my phone call before you send that e-mail. Our plan is still top secret.

Greg: But, but …

SCENE 10. INTERIOR. JOSH'S/MAYA'S BEDROOMS. DAY.

Split scene: Maya is in bed and is still sleeping. Josh is sitting at his desk and calls her on his mobile.

Maya: *(Her mobile rings. She wakes up and answers.)* Hello?

---

11 **to go mental** [gəʊ 'mentl] verrückt werden • 12 **collection point** [kə'lekʃn pɔɪnt] Sammelstelle • 13 **central** ['sentrl] zentral

Josh: Secretary Maya?

Maya: Huh? Josh? It's six o'clock on Saturday morning!

Josh: Secretary Maya … .

Maya: And why can't you just call me Maya?

Josh: Because these instructions are important, Maya … I mean Secretary Maya.

Maya: Why are you calling so early, Josh?

Josh: It's time!

Maya: Oh, it's time to send the e-mails about … ?

Josh: Shhh! It's top secret!

Maya: Hmmm. But Greg wasn't too happy that his house is our collection point. Are you sure about this, Josh?

Josh: Yes, I'm sure. Now, listen carefully, Secretary Maya. This is your Chairperson speaking! Go to your laptop! *(pauses)* Well, are you there yet?

Maya: *(still in bed, laughs to herself)* Um … wait a minute, Chairperson, sir! I'm getting up.

Goes to her desk where there is a laptop. A hamster cage is next to it.

Josh: Are you at your laptop, ready for instructions?

Maya: *(trying not to laugh)* Yes, my Chairperson!

Josh: *(hears a noise that sounds like someone is scratching)* Huh? What's that noise? Someone's listening in on us!

Maya: It's OK … er … it's Elvis.

Josh: Elvis?

Maya: Elvis, my hamster.

Josh: Oh, OK … . Now, are you ready?

Maya: Yes!

Josh: Send out the e-mails … NOW!

5 **instruction** [ɪn'strʌkʃn] Anweisung • 10 **Shhh!** [ʃ] Pst! • 13 **to listen carefully** [ˌlɪsn ˈkeəfli] gut zuhören • 15 **to pause** [pɔ:z] zögern • 16 **to laugh to oneself** [ˌlɑ:f tə wʌn'self] in sich hineingrinsen • 18 **cage** [keɪdʒ] Käfig • 23 **to listen in on** [lɪsn‿'ɪn ɒn] (heimlich) mithören

SCENE 11. EXTERIOR. STREET. DAY.

Josh, Havana and Maya are walking to Greg's house on their way to school.

JOSH: *(to Havana)* On Saturday I gave the instruction to send over 500 e-mails out to everyone we know.

HAVANA: Great, guys! I wonder if anybody has brought their unwanted clothes?

JOSH: We'll soon see!

They arrive at Greg's house.

MAYA: Wow! Look at all those bags of clothes!

At that moment Greg's dad comes out the front door. He looks around the front garden.

GREG'S DAD: W-what's all this?... *(angry)* Greg! Come out here this minute!

Josh, Maya and Havana run off.

---

10 **front door** [frʌnt 'dɔ:] Haustür • 11 **to look around** [lʊk‿ə'raʊnd] sich umschauen

SCENE 12. INTERIOR. JOSH'S BEDROOM. DAY.

Rubbish bags full of old clothes are everywhere in Josh's room. Josh and Havana are sitting on the floor between them. They look disappointed.

GREG: *(enters the room with a big bag of clothes)* Sorry I'm late for the meeting! *(He puts the bag on Josh's bed).* Here you are, Josh!

JOSH: Ugh! Not on my bed!

GREG: There are plastic bags of old clothes everywhere in our house! In the garage, in the living room. In my bedroom! And people are bringing more! There's no more room!

JOSH: *(picking up the bag from the bed)* Did you have to put them on my bed, Greg? I have to sleep there tonight! Ugh! These clothes are all wet!

MAYA: *(comes in quickly, talking)* Sorry I'm late! *(She falls over a bag of clothes.)* Oh! What are we going to do we do with all these old clothes?

GREG: Hmmm. That's what Mum and Dad keep asking me!

MAYA: We don't have a shop … .

HAVANA: No, but we could open a stall!

MAYA: Cool! A clothes stall!

JOSH: Yes, we can start with a clothes stall, but one day it could become a shop, then two shops, then three shops … . We could have shops in Paris, Tokyo, New York … .

MAYA: Josh, be realistic! We're talking about a charity, not a designer jeans shop.

HAVANA: I'll ask Mrs Burns if we can have a stall in the playground after school, maybe Friday?

---

3 **disappointed** [ˌdɪsəˈpɔɪntɪd] enttäuscht • 11 **room** [ruːm] *(hier)* Platz • 18 **to keep asking** [kiːp ˈɑːskɪŋ] andauernd (nach)fragen • 20 **to open** [ˈəʊpn] aufmachen

SCENE 13. EXTERIOR. SCHOOL. DAY.

The four friends have opened a clothes stall in the school playground. Pupils are buying clothes.

FIRST BUYER: How much is this pullover?

MAYA: It's 25p.

SECOND BUYER: What about this cool scarf?

MAYA: All the clothes are 25p.

FIRST BUYER: That's cheap, I'll take it.

SECOND BUYER: Me too. Here's the money.

MAYA: Thank you. The money all goes to make a difference in Africa.

MAYA: *(looks up when she hears thunder)* Uh-oh! That was thunder!

GREG: If it rains … we're in trouble!

MRS BURNS: Wow! What a lovely poster, Havana.

HAVANA: Oh, thanks, Mrs Burns.

MRS BURNS: This is wonderful, all of you! (*She gives them a big black plastic bag of clothes.)* Here you are! You'll be

9 **to go to** [ˈɡəʊ tə] ist bestimmt für • 11 **thunder** [ˈθʌndə] Donner • 13 **to be in trouble** [bi ɪn ˈtrʌbl] in Schwierigkeiten sein

happy to hear that I've brought you all my unwanted clothes! They've been in my wardrobe for 10 years! Styles change so fast and I don't want to look old-fashioned!

JOSH and MAYA: More clothes? Er … um … thank you, Miss.

MRS BURNS: You're welcome! There are some lovely skirts in there, oh, and my favourite shorts. I'm sure someone's mum will buy them!

Mrs Burns leaves. Maya takes out the shorts from her bag and shows Josh. They are huge. Josh makes a horrified face when he sees them. Sound of thunder again. They all look up.

JOSH: Uh-oh … rain! Quick! Committee members! We have to take all the clothes inside!

MAYA: But where? The school building is already closed!

HAVANA: What can we do? It's raining!

JOSH: We'll have to take the clothes back to our collection point!

GREG: Quick, to the collection point! Huh? Wait! That's my house!

JOSH: I'm sorry. Greg, but it's closest!

GREG: *(horrified)* Oh no! Now my parents will really go mental!

SCENE 14. INTERIOR. GREG'S HOUSE. DAY.

Sound of thunder and rain outside. The committee members are all in blankets. They are sitting at the kitchen table. Maya sneezes.

GREG'S MUM: *(comes in with cups of hot chocolate)* Bless you, Maya! Here, drink this, all of you.

MAYA: Thanks, a hot drink is just what we all need.

JOSH, HAVANA, GREG: Yeah, thanks!

10 **horrified** ['hɒrɪfaɪd] entsetzt • 10 **to make a face** [ˌmeɪk‿ə 'feɪs] eine Grimasse schneiden • 20 **closest** ['kləʊsɪst] am nächsten • 24 **blanket** ['blæŋkɪt] Decke • 25 **to sneeze** [sni:z] niesen • 26 **Bless you!** ['bles ju] Gesundheit!

Mum: You're all welcome. It's too bad about the rain.

Josh: *(to Greg's mum)* We're really sorry we had to bring all the clothes back to your house again.

Mum: What else could you do with them? But I hope it won't be for a long time … . How many did you sell?

Greg: Almost nothing, Mum. It started to rain almost as soon as we opened the stall.

Greg's mum shakes her head sympathetically as she leaves.

Maya: Committee members! *(Maya sneezes again.)*

All: Bless you!

Maya: Thanks! I think we need a Plan B.

Josh: I have a brilliant Plan B!

Maya: *(worried)* Uh-oh!

Josh: We can't sell the clothes, right?

All: Right!

Josh: So, why don't we … *(dramatically)* send them to Africa?

Greg: Get real, Josh! It's too hot in Africa to wear pullovers and scarves!

Maya: That's not true, Greg. Remember the film we saw? Some parts of Africa have very cold winters. People there need warm clothes, too.

Havana: That's true. But how on earth do we get all the stuff to Africa?

Josh: Er … by ship.

All: By ship?

Josh: Yes. It's slower than by plane, so it's much cheaper.

Havana: By ship or by plane, it will still cost money. How much have we raised so far, Greg?

Greg: We've raised … *(opens the donations box and counts)* only £1.20.

Maya and **Havana**: What? That's all!

---

8 **sympathetically** [ˌsɪmpəˈθetɪkli] mitleidsvoll • 11 **Plan B** [plæn ˈbiː] Plan B / alternativer Plan • 16 **dramatically** [drəˈmætɪkli] dramatisch • 23 **How on earth** [haʊ ɒn ˈɜːθ] wie in aller Welt • 29 **so far** [səʊ ˈfɑː] bis jetzt

Josh: Hmmm. I have another idea!

Maya: Oh no … plan C? Here we go again.

Greg: What's your idea, Josh?

Josh: *(thinking while he talks)* Secretary Maya, please write this letter … .

Maya: No way! I sent all those e-mails and now we have mountains of smelly old clothes!

Greg: Smelly old *wet* clothes! We have to do something! I'm the chairperson's personal assistant, I'll write it.

Greg takes off his blanket and sits at the laptop.

Josh: Thanks, Personal Assistant … . "Dear Richard – "

Greg: Huh? Richard? Who am I writing to?

Josh: No, no, start again … . "Dear Sir Richard Branson –"

Greg: Wow! I'm writing to Sir Richard Branson? He's the President of Virgin Atlantic Airways!

Josh: *(thinking)* "We know you'll want to help our charity make a difference in Africa … ."

Greg: *(writing on the laptop)* Wait, Josh! You're going too fast!

Josh: "We hope one of your jumbo jets can take the clothes we have collected for the poor in Africa … ."

SCENE 15. EXTERIOR. OUTSIDE GREG'S HOUSE. DAY.

Greg and his mum are putting the last bags of unwanted clothes in the car. Greg is very worried and unhappy. Greg's dad has just got into the car and is looking around.

Greg's mum: *(to Dad)* OK, those are the last bags!

Greg's dad: Finally! It looks like a garden again!

Greg: *(worried)* Oh, what will the others say when they find out!

---

2 **Here we go again.** [hɪə wi ˈɡəʊ əˌɡen] Jetzt geht das schon wieder los. • 6 **No way!** [nəʊ ˈweɪ] Auf keinen Fall! • 7 **smelly** [ˈsmeli] übel riechend • 13 **Branson** [ˈbrænsn] • 15 **Virgin Atlantic Airways** [ˌvɜːdʒɪn ətˈlæntɪk ˌeəweɪz] *britische Fluggesellschaft* • 24 **to get into** [get‿ˈɪntə] einsteigen

Mum: I'm sorry love, but we absolutely could not keep all those wet clothes in the house another day! It was beginning to smell very musty!

Dad: And I don't want more neighbours to complain that it looks like a rubbish dump in our garden! How embarrassing!

Greg: But we would have only needed to wait another week! I'm sure Josh would have got an answer from Virgin Atlantic by then.

Mum: Sorry, love, but we couldn't wait longer. Dad will take the clothes to the charity shop. The shop will sell them, and the money will still go to help the poor.

Greg: It's not the same. We wanted *our* charity to make a difference in Africa!

Mum: I know, and you've all worked very hard, love. Dad and I are very proud of you … aren't we, dear? (*looks at Greg's dad pointedly)*

Dad: Yes, we are, but Greg, you can't change the world in a day!

1 love [lʌv] Schatz, Liebling • **1 absolutely not** [ˌæbsəˈluːtli ˈnɒt] auf keinen Fall • **3 musty** [ˈmʌsti] moderig • **5 rubbish dump** [ˈrʌbɪʃ dʌmp] Mülldeponie • **7 would have** [ˈwʊd həv] hätten • **16 proud** [praʊd] stolz • **17 pointedly** [ˈpɔɪntɪdli] spitz

Greg: So do we just say it's too hard, and give up?

Mum: No ... but Africa is a big continent! Maybe you've bitten off more than you can chew ... .

Greg: Huh? Bitten off more than we can chew? Like when you're so hungry you take a huge bite of a hamburger, but it's –

Mum: *(laughs)* More than even *you* can chew, Greg! Maybe you kids can think of another way to make a difference?

SCENE 16. EXTERIOR. THE PARK. DAY.

The committee is sitting in the park under a tree.

Maya: Everyone is here for another meeting. We still haven't solved the problem. What do we do with all the stuff at Greg's house?

Josh: *(to Greg)* The committee understands your problem, Personal Assistant. We know the clothes are blocking up your front hall and your living room.

Greg looks worried.

Maya: And his garage.

Havana: And your bedroom, right, Greg?

Greg looks more worried.

Josh: But Greg, please look after those clothes for just a few more days.

Maya: Africa needs them, Greg!

Greg: Hey, guys ... er ... the stuff's ... gone.

Josh: What? What do you mean it's gone?

Greg: Gone. The clothes are gone ... .

All: What?

---

2 **continent** [ˈkɒntɪnənt] Kontinent • 3 **to bite off more than one can chew** [baɪt ˌˈɒf ˌmɔː ðn wʌn kæn ˈtʃuː] sich übernehmen, sich zu viel zumuten • 15 **to block up** [blɒk ˈʌp] verstopfen

GREG: I'm sorry, I feel really bad … Mum said the whole house smelled, Dad said the garden looked like a rubbish dump … they both said everything had to go. But Dad took the clothes to a charity shop, so it will still make a difference … .

JOSH: *Which* charity shop did your dad take them to?

GREG: *(closes his eyes and pauses)* Oxfam.

JOSH: The enemy! You gave it to *them*!

MAYA: Stop it, Josh! Oxfam is *not* the enemy! And we're not in competition with them! We all have the same goal!

JOSH: *(angry)* Yeah, Maya, but how does CA$H raise money if we've got nothing to sell?

HAVANA: We can raise money if we busk! You know, play a musical instrument in the street?

GREG: Ha! No one would give money to hear me play my guitar!

MAYA: Hmmm … maybe not. But Havana's a brilliant dancer! And Josh, hasn't your mum got a CD of some cool African drums? Havana can dance to that!

JOSH: and **GREG:** But get real, Maya!

MAYA: No buts, guys. Let's do this!

JOSH: *(angry)* Hey, I'm the Chairperson, Maya!

GREG: Where shall we do it? And when?

HAVANA: In the park on Saturday morning!

JOSH: OK, let's vote. Who thinks we should busk this Saturday morning in the park?

Maya raises her hand first. Havana follows. Greg and Josh look at each other then raise their hands too.

JOSH: The Committee has decided!

HAVANA: Great. Let's busk and raise a lot of cash for CA$H. Hey! Cash for CA$H!

They all laugh and feel better.

---

9 **to be in competition with** [bi ɪn ˌkɒmpəˈtɪʃn wɪð] mit jmdm. konkurrieren • 10 **goal** [gəʊl] Ziel • 13 **to busk** [bʌsk] Straßenmusik machen • 21 **no buts** [nəʊ ˈbʌts] keine Wiederrede

SCENE 17. EXTERIOR. THE PARK. DAY.

The four friends are in the park. Havana is in the background and is dancing to a CD of African drums. Maya, Greg and Josh are collecting money.

YOUNG BOY: *(walks over to Maya, Greg and Josh)* Well done! Africa needs all the help it can get! Here's my donation. *(He puts some money in a box and walks away.)*

JOSH: Thank you! *(to Maya and Greg)* This is great, we're going to collect hundreds for Africa!

WOMAN: *(walks over to the three and reads the sign with a critical expression)* CA$H? Oh really? Where's your charity licence then?

GREG: Sorry?

WOMAN: Before I give you a donation, I want to be sure you have a licence to collect people's money!

MAYA: A licence?

WOMAN: Does CA$H have a licence or not?

JOSH and **GREG:** *(nervous)* Er … n-no.

WOMAN: I thought not! So how do I know you're going to spend my money on Africa? How do I know you're not going to spend it on sweets or fast food?

2 background ['bækgraʊnd] Hintergrund • **10 critical expression** [ˌkrɪtɪkl ɪk'spreʃn] skeptischer Blick • **11 licence** ['laɪsns] Genehmigung • **11 then** [ðen] dann • **12 Sorry?** ['sɒri] Wie bitte? / Entschuldigung?

Maya: Oh! But we would never –

Woman: And do you even have headquarters?

Greg: *(smiles proudly)* Yes, we have headquarters.

Woman: *(She takes out a pen and paper.)* Where are they?

Josh: *(worried)* The headquarters are my bedroom … .

Woman: What! Make a difference to Africa? More like make a difference to your pocket money! I'm going to report you kids to the police!

The woman walks off. Greg turns off the CD player. Maya and Josh quickly take down the poster.

Greg: Come on, Havana!

Havana: *(still dancing)* Hey! I was dancing to that. Have we collected enough money already?

Greg: *(worried)* No, Havana! But we have to go now! She's reporting us to the police!

Maya, Josh and Greg run off.

Havana: What? Police? Why? Guys! Wait!

Havana follows the others.

SCENE 18. INTERIOR. MAYA'S HOUSE. NIGHT.

Maya and Gran are doing the washing up.

Gran: What is it Maya, dear? You seem worried about something.

Maya: Oh, it's nothing, Gran.

Gran: What about that wonderful charity you and your friends started?

Maya: Ugh!

Gran: Oh, I see. Is that the problem, dear?

Maya: *(frustrated)* Oh Gran, it's all gone wrong! We sent out e-mails to hundreds of people and we got too many

---

6 **more like** ['mɔː laɪk] eher wie • 7 **to report sb** [rɪ'pɔːt] jmdn. anzeigen • 11 **Come on!** [kʌm‿'ɒn] Komm jetzt! / Komm schon!

unwanted clothes and people brought more and more and then it rained on our stall so the clothes all got wet and smelly and Virgin Atlantic haven't answered and Sebastiano hasn't answered either and we tried to busk in the park to raise money but we don't have a licence and a woman is going to report us to the police.... !

GRAN: *(very confused)* But I thought your friend's name was Josh, not Sebastiano ... .

Maya starts to cry.

GRAN: *(She puts her arms around Maya.)* Oh, my poor dear! I didn't know you were asking people for money in the park!

MAYA: The woman's going to report us to the police!

GRAN: I'll call the Town Hall and ask them about a licence. But, you know, maybe you should try to make a difference a little closer to home ... .

MAYA: Closer to home? What do you mean, Gran?

GRAN: Well, for a start you could help your old Gran do the washing up!

They laugh.

GRAN: Start small and who knows? You know what they say: Out of little acorns, great oaks grow. Now, hand me those dirty plates, dear ... .

Maya just stands there for a minute and thinks.

GRAN: Maya?

MAYA: Oh, sorry Gran, I was thinking about what you said about starting small. And helping people people closer to home ... .

7 confused [kən'fju:zd] verwirrt • **14 Town Hall** [taʊn 'hɔ:l] Rathaus • **16 closer** ['kləʊsə] näher • **22 out of** ['aʊt͜əv] aus • **22 acorn** ['eɪkɔ:n] Eichel • **22 oak** [əʊk] Eiche • **22 to grow** [grəʊ] wachsen

SCENE 19. INTERIOR. JOSH'S BEDROOM. DAY.

Maya is at the laptop. The others are sitting on the floor and on Josh's bed. The bags of clothes are all gone now.

JOSH: OK, everyone is here! The Committee meeting can begin. How much money have we raised, Personal Assistant?

GREG: *(opens the donation box excitedly)* The grand total is … *(disappointed)* £3.50!

JOSH: That's all? So much work for so little money! Ugh!

MAYA: Look guys, we've had a lot of problems, but are we going to give up?

JOSH, HAVANA, and GREG look at the floor and do not answer.

MAYA: *(louder)* I said are we going to give up?

JOSH, HAVANA, GREG: NO!

MAYA: That's better! Listen, I have another plan. Mr Chairperson.

JOSH: We've had Plan A, Plan B and Plan C, so this must be … Plan D?

MAYA: I want to have a committee meeting tonight at my house.

JOSH: But Maya, the CA$H headquarters are in my room!

MAYA: I know, but I want you to hear what my gran has to say about –

JOSH: Oh, come on, Maya! Do we really have to listen to your grandmother? No offence, but what can an old lady tell us?

MAYA: Old people can have some very interesting ideas, Josh! My house at 8:00 everybody!

GREG: But Maya, I've got football tonight.

MAYA: *(smiling)* My gran is making flapjacks, Greg … .

---

6 **grand total** [grænd 'təʊtl] Gesamtsumme • 8 **so little** [səʊ 'lɪtl] so wenig • 24 **Come on!** [kʌm‿'ɒn] Jetzt hör aber auf! • 25 **No offence** [nəʊ ə'fens] Nichts für ungut • 30 **flapjack** ['flæpdʒæk] Müsliriegel

GREG: But … but …

MAYA: Gran's special flapjacks with lots of honey. Mmmm! You love Gran's flapjacks, Greg … .

GREG: *(dreaming)* Mmmm … flapjacks. I'll be there at eight.

SCENE 20. INTERIOR. MAYA'S HOUSE. NIGHT.

The committee is sitting around the kitchen table. A kitchen whiteboard and a clock are hanging on the wall near them. Everyone has just finished eating flapjacks. There is one flapjack left on the plate in the middle of the table.

GREG: Mmmm. Maya, your gran's flapjacks are much better than football practice. Can I have the last one, guys? I'm starv- … *(He stops himself before he says it.)*

MAYA: *(laughing)* Help yourself, Greg!

Maya's gran comes in with her handbag and puts it on the floor.

GRAN: Hello everybody. *(She sees the empty plate on the table.)* Oh, I see you liked my flapjacks!

GREG: They were wonderful, thank you!

MAYA: Hey Gran … please tell them what you told me.

GRAN: What did I tell you?

MAYA: You know!

GRAN: All I said was sometimes to be successful you have to start small … .

JOSH: Start small?

GRAN: That's right, Josh. *(She goes to the whiteboard, picks up a pen and draws something)*

GRAN: Who can tell me what this is?

GREG: Hmm … er … something Maya's hamster did?

They laugh.

---

2 **honey** [ˈhʌni] Honig • 13 **Help yourself!** [help jɔːˈself] Bedien dich!

Havana: Is it a nut?

Gran: No, not exactly, Havana.

Josh: A fat man with a funny hat?

Gran: No, Josh, it isn't. I'll tell you: It's an acorn.

Gran draws a large tree coming out of the acorn. She writes "acorn" and "great oak".

Maya: *(to her friends)* Don't you see…? "Out of little acorns, great oaks grow!"

All: Huh?

Maya: I was telling Gran all about CA$H and all our problems and that's what she said … .

Havana: Oh, I see. It means we have to start small!

Gran: Exactly.

Maya: We won't make any difference at all if we bite off more than we can chew …

Greg: *(He is about to take another bite of his flapjack and stops.)* That's funny, that's what my mum said …

---

1 nut [nʌt] Nuss • **16 to take another bite** [teɪk‿əˌnʌðə 'baɪt] nochmal abbeißen

Gran: So maybe you can start by making a difference closer to home? Maya made a big difference for me a few days ago.

Josh: Huh? What did she do?

Gran: Oh, she helped me do the washing up!

They all laugh.

Maya: Seriously! I'm sure there are lots of other people who we can help right here in Greenwich.

Havana: Yeah, older people who live alone find some things difficult to do.

Gran: Young mothers often need help, too.

Josh: We could help people in their gardens.

Greg: And in their homes.

Gran: *(picks up her handbag, takes a piece of paper out of it and puts it on the table)* If you're going to ask people for money, you'll need this … .

Josh/Greg/Havana: What is it?

Maya: *(to her friends)* Cool! This tells us how we can get a licence so no one can report us to the police! *(hugs Gran)* Thanks Gran!

Gran: *(looks at the clock)* Oh, eight thirty! Time for that TV documentary I want to watch.

All: Thanks for everything!

Gran: Good luck, kids!

Gran leaves.

Josh: *(to himself)* A TV documentary? *(pauses)* That's it! Why didn't I think of it before! *(to Maya)* I'm sorry, Maya, I was wrong about your grandmother.

Maya: *(surprised)* Huh?

Josh: She's just given me a brilliant idea! We can make a documentary film of how we help people!

Maya: What a brainwave, Josh!

---

7 **seriously** [ˈsɪəriəsli] im Ernst • 9 **to find sth difficult** [faɪnd ˈdɪfɪklt] sich mit etw. schwer tun • 19 **to hug sb** [hʌg] jmdn. umarmen • 22 **documentary** [ˌdɒkjəˈmentri] Dokumentarfilm • 26 **That's it!** [ðætsˈɪt] Genau!

Havana: I can make a poster to show what we do.
Greg: And the people we help can make a donation!
Josh: Maybe Mrs Burns will let us show the documentary to our class. Come on guys, we're going to make a film!
All: A film! HOORAY!

They all start to jump up and down.

SCENE 21. EXTERIOR. STREET. DAY.

The CA$H committee is filming interviews with people in Greenwich High Street. Maya is asking passers-by questions. Around them are an OLD LADY, OLD MAN, A HOUSWIFE, A BLIND GIRL, A YOUNG MOTHER, AND A YOUNG MAN.

Maya: Thanks for your participation. We're doing some research about how we can make a difference in Greenwich. Is everyone ready for a few questions?

5 **Hooray!** [hʊˈreɪ] Hurra! • 8 **passer-by** [ˌpɑːsəˈbaɪ] Passant/-in • 12 **participation** [pɑːˌtɪsɪˈpeɪʃn] Teilnahme

Everyone: Of course / Yes / Certainly / Go ahead.

Maya: *(to the OLD LADY)* What would make a difference to your life? What do you really need?

Old lady: Well, I'm 77 and I live alone. I often need help. For example, just now I need someone to help me in my garden. That would make a big difference!

Maya: *(to the HOUSEWIFE)* What would make a difference for you?

Housewife: I haven't got a computer. I need someone to look things up for me on the Internet.

Maya: *(to the BLIND GIRL, touches her arm)* How about you?

Blind Girl: I love films, but I'm blind. I'd like someone to watch films with me and describe what I can't see. That would make a big difference to me!

Maya: *(to the OLD MAN)* And you, sir?

Old man: I was always a big reader, but now my eyes are not so good. I can't always find the books I like on tape. I'd like someone to record books for me on a tape recorder so I can listen later.

Young mother: Oh, some help would make a big difference! I have two small children and a big dog. I have no time to take Prince for a walk.

Young man: I work so hard I have no time to clean my car. It would make a difference if someone cleaned it for me!

Maya: Thank you very much. I'm sure CA$H can help you all!

---

1 of course [əv 'kɔ:s] natürlich • **1 certainly** ['sɜ:tnli] selbstverständlich • **1 Go ahead.** [gəʊ ə'hed] Nur zu. • **5 just** [dʒʌst] gerade eben • **10 to look up** [lʊk‿'ʌp] nachschauen • **18 tape** [teɪp] Kassette

SCENE 22. INTERIOR. JOSH'S BEDROOM. NIGHT.

The committee is sitting around the room and Maya is holding the donation box. Josh is editing the film on his laptop. They are all tired and very happy.

MAYA: *(holds the donation box towards the others)* Does anyone have more donations? I can't wait to see how much we've raised after a week of hard work!

HAVANA: Well, I just got £2 for babysitting for one neighbour … and I got £2 for walking another neighbour's dog. *(puts money in the box)* The silly dog ran away, but I found him in the end!

JOSH: I know, it's all here in the film! *(points to his video camera)*

GREG: I just cut my grandfather's grass. It was hard work! but he gave me a £4 donation … and a £2 tip! *(He puts the money in the box.)*

MAYA: Yesterday I watched a DVD with the blind girl that we interviewed. *(puts her money in the box)* I described everything I saw for her. It was a great film, and we've become friends.

JOSH: *(takes money from his pocket)* And here's the rest of the money we all raised from washing cars, selling flapjacks and washing windows.

MAYA: OK, everybody, let's hear the grand total! *(She opens the box, dumps the money out on the floor and counts it.)* That's £66.25 in just one week!

GREG: Wow! Let's take it to Oxfam first thing tomorrow!

MAYA: Imagine the school books or medicine it can buy!

JOSH: Well done everyone! We've made a difference to people in Greenwich and Africa!

ALL: HOORAY!

---

2 to edit [ˈedɪt] schneiden • **10 in the end** [ɪn ði‿ˈend] schließlich, zum Schluss • **14 tip** [tɪp] Trinkgeld • **24 to dump sth out** [ˈdʌmp … aʊt] etw. ausschütten • **26 first thing** [ˌfɜːst ˈθɪŋ] als Allererstes

Josh's mobile phone rings. He answers it.

JOSH: Hello? *(to the others)* Shhh! I can't hear! *(He moves away to one side.)*

GREG: *(to Havana and Maya)* That was great! I must say, I never thought we could do it!

MAYA/HAVANA: We always knew we could!

GREG: And we didn't even need help from … Sebastiano! Ha ha!

HAVANA: *(laughs)* Oh Greg! You're just jealous!

JOSH *(on the phone)* We can, Mrs Burns …? Really …? Oh! Thank you! *(Josh comes back to the others.)*

MAYA: *(talking to Havana and Greg)* £66.25! It couldn't get any better … .

JOSH: *(closing his phone and smiling)* It just did! That was Mrs Burns. She says we can show our film next week!

MAYA: Wow! To the whole class?

JOSH: No. To the whole school!

They all jump up and hug each other.

ALL: HOORAY!

9 **jealous** ['dʒeləs] eifersüchtig • 12 **not … any** [nɒt 'eni] gar nicht • 14 **It just did!** [ɪt ˌdʒʌst 'dɪd] *(hier)* Und ob! • 16 **whole** [həʊl] ganze/-r

Exercise

Who said what?

Who says these lines? Who do they say them to and why?

Example: "Last night I had too many chips … I couldn't eat them all. So I threw them away. Now I feel bad … ."
Maya says this to her friends after she sees the film about famine in Africa.

1. "Well, Josh, I thought you wanted to be a famous film director … ."
2. "Hey! Who turned the lights off?"
3. "When the earth gets hotter, Africa really feels it."
4. "Imagine, if he had stayed there, I could be one of those kids!"
5. "Huh? Josh? It's six o'clock on Saturday morning!"
6. "How do I know you're not going to spend it on sweets or fast food?"
7. "Oh, come on, Maya! Do we really have to listen to your grandmother? No offence, but what can an old lady tell us?"
8. "Mmmm … flapjacks. I'll be there at eight."
9. "If you're going to ask people for money, you'll need this … ."
10. "For example, just now I need someone to help me in my garden."

A group project: Making a film

The following tasks and exercises should help you to film 'Make a difference'.

1. A checklist

1. Work in groups of 5 to 8. Read scene 1. On the next page is a list of tasks to help you film the scene.

Getting ready

a) *Choose a director, and give reasons for your choice. (There can also be more than one director.)*
b) *Decide who should have which part, and why.*
c) *Choose people who will decide on camera, light and sound effects. Why did you make your choices?*
d) *Decide which props and costumes you need to collect. Where can you find these things?*
e) *Decide what you need to make the set for this scene. Does the scene take place inside or outside?*

Acting

f) *Actors learn your lines and practise the scene together. Find the words that are difficult for you, and practise them. How can you remember the words? Practise any gestures or expressions that you need for this scene.*

Filming

g) *Decide which camera, light and/or sound effects you will need and how to do them. Look at p. 44 for information about camera techniques. For light and sound effects, think about when and where this scene takes place, the weather, and if anything that happens makes noise.*

2. *Now act and film the scene together.*

3. *Use this checklist for each scene you want to film.*

director [dɪˈrektə] Regisseur • **prop** [prɒp] Requisite • **to take place** [teɪk ˈpleɪs] stattfinden • **lines** [laɪnz] Text • **gesture** [ˈdʒestʃə] Geste • **expression** [ɪkˈspreʃn] Gesichtsausdruck • **camera technique** [ˈkæmrə tekˌniːk] Kameratechnik

2. Using your camera techniques

Match the pictures with the descriptions below.

1. 

2. 

3. 

4. 

a) **Long shot** shows actors, objects from far away and a lot of the picture around them. This shot helps to show the context of the scene.

b) **Medium shot** shows an actor's upper body. Good for dialogues because it focuses on actions and the actors.

c) **Close-up** shows a small part of the scene, for example the actor's shoulders and head. There is focus on one person or thing.

d) **Zoom (in or out)** using the camera to get closer to and focus in on an actor or object (zoom in) or to move away (zoom out) so you can see other scene details.

---

shot [ʃɒt] Aufnahme • **upper body** [ˌʌpə ˈbɒdi] Oberkörper • **action** [ˈækʃn] *hier:* Bewegung • **close-up** [ˈkləʊsʌp] Nahaufnahme • **shoulder** [ˈʃəʊldə] Schulter • **Zoom in / out** [zuːm ˈɪn; zuːm ˈaʊt] heranzoomen / wegzoomen • **to focus in on** [ˌfəʊkəs ˈɪn‿ɒn] in den Mittelpunkt stellen • **detail** [ˈdiːteɪl] Detail

3. Showing emotions and reactions

a) *Sometimes the actor has to show an emotion through body language or an expression. Work with a partner. Each of you chooses a list. Then choose an emotion or reaction and act it. See if your partner can guess what you want to show.*

A	B
a) worried	a) dreaming
b) thinking	b) surprised
c) laughing	c) horrified
d) angry	d) very confused
e) happy	e) trying not to laugh

b) *The script sometimes tells actors how to say a line. With a partner, practise saying these lines. Then compare your lines with one other group.*

a) *(suddenly happy)* That's the bell for lunch! (p. 8)
b) *(thinking)* Hmmm ... make a film and make a difference. But how? (p. 9)
c) *(laughing)* Mum! Hello! Er ... you're talking to the cat again! (p. 10)
d) *(excited)* Guys, listen! (p. 13)
e) *(dreaming)* Hmmm. Our own charity! (p. 15)
g) *(to himself)* Oh nooo. Now what have I started ... ? (p. 19)
i) W-what's all this?... *(angry)* Greg! Come out here this minute! (p. 22)
k) *(nervous)* Er ... n-no. (p. 31)
o) The grand total is ... *(disappointed)* £3.50! (p. 34)

reaction [ri'ækʃn] Reaktion • **body language** ['bɒdi ˌlæŋgwɪdʒ] Körpersprache

4. Practising actions

The script sometimes tells actors the actions they must do.

Practise these in a group, then compare your actions with one other group. When you are doing these actions, think about the situation, the character(s) doing them, and what they may be feeling or thinking.

1. *Greg runs off. The others look surprised and shake their heads. (p. 8)*
2. *At that moment Greg's dad comes out the front door. He looks around the front garden. (p. 22)*
3. *Maya takes out the shorts from her bag and shows Josh. They are huge. Josh makes a horrified face when he sees them. Sound of thunder. They all look up. (p. 25)*
4. *The woman walks off. Greg turns off the CD player. Maya and Josh quickly take down the poster. (p. 32)*

5. A review

After you have read 'Make a Difference' and filmed a scene/scenes, write a review of the script and describe your experience. Think about these things:

- main characters in 'Make a Difference'
- summary of the plot
- your favourite character(s) and why you like him/her/them
- character(s) you didn't like as much, and why
- favourite part of the story and why you like it
- part(s) of the story you didn't like so much, and why
- if you liked making a film or not, and why
- what you liked the most about making a film
- what was the most difficult thing about making a film
- if you would make another film or not, and why

review [rɪˈvjuː] Rezension, Kritik • **plot** [plɒt] Handlung

Solutions

Before you read the script

1. The title

a) Possible solutions: to try to help other people, to try to do something good for your town, to try to make your world better

b) –

2. Cover picture –

3. The characters

a) Maya b) Josh c) Greg d) Maya e) Maya / Havana f) Greg
g) Josh h) Greg i) Josh j) Havana

4. What is Oxfam?

charity / poor / *(see 'Emergencies' or 'Where we work')* / second-hand clothes / *(see 'Donate')* money / food / medicine.

5. Sounds in dialogues –

Exercise

Who said what?

1. Josh's mother says this to Josh to suggest that he should make a film and make a difference. (p. 9)
2. The Coach says this after Greg turned off the lights in the locker room and the Coach was still in there. (p. 12)
3. This is a line from the film and is said twice, first by Havana, and then by Greg, Havana and Maya. First Havana says this to Greg when she explains why it is important for Africa for him to turn off the lights. Then Greg, Havana and Maya say this to explain to Josh why Greg is turning off the lights. (pp. 11, 13)
4. Josh says this to Maya, Havana and Greg to explain to them why he has a special reason to be unhappy about the situation in Africa. (p. 13)
5. Maya says this to Josh to complain when he calls her very early to tell her she should send the e-mails. (p. 21)

6. The woman in the park says this to Josh, Maya, and Greg when she finds out that they want to collect money, but they don't have a licence. She doesn't believe that they are really collecting money for Africa. (p. 31)
7. Josh says this to Maya when she wants Josh, Havana and Greg to come to her house for a meeting so that her grandmother can tell them her idea. He isn't happy about this. (p. 34)
8. Greg says this to Maya. He has changed his mind and now (because of the flapjacks) he'll come to Maya's house for the meeting although he has football practice at the same time. (p. 35)
9. Gran says this to Maya and the others. She gives them information from the Town Hall so that they can get a licence and collect money without any problem. (p. 37)
10. The old woman that Maya interviews says this. She says this to tell Maya what would make a difference in her life. (p. 39)

A group project: Making a film

1. **A checklist** –
2. **Using your camera techniques**
   1.b / 2.d / 3.c / 4.a
3. **Showing emotions and reactions** –
4. **Practising actions** –
5. **A review** –